# FACE to FACE

# THE DREAMSEEKER POETRY SERIES

Books in the DreamSeeker Poetry Series, intended to make available fine writing by Anabaptist-related poets, are published by Cascadia Publishing House under the DreamSeeker Books imprint and often copublished with Herald Press. Cascadia oversees content of these poetry collections in collaboration with the DreamSeeker Poetry Series Editor Jeff Gundy (Jean Janzen volumes 1-4) as well as in consultation with its Editorial Council and the authors themselves.

Also worth noting are two poetry collections that would likely have been included in the series had it been in existence then:

# FACE to FACE

*A Poetry Collection*

## Julie Cadwallader-Staub

**DreamSeeker Poetry Series, Volume 8**

**DreamSeeker Books**
TELFORD, PENNSYLVANIA

*an imprint of*
Cascadia Publishing House LLC

**Cascadia Publishing House orders, information, reprint permissions:**
contact@CascadiaPublishingHouse.com
1-215-723-9125
126 Klingerman Road, Telford PA 18969
www.CascadiaPublishingHouse.com

*Face to Face*
Copyright © 2010 by Cascadia Publishing House, Telford, PA 18969
DreamSeeker Books is an imprint of Cascadia Publishing House LLC
Library of Congress Catalog Number: 2010017657
**ISBN 13:** 978-1-931038-52-2; **ISBN 10:** 1-931038-52-X
Book design by Cascadia Publishing House
Cover design by Gwen M. Stamm

The paper used in this publication is recycled and meets the
minimum requirements of American National Standard for Information
Sciences—Permanence of Paper for Printed Library Materials, ANSI Z39.48-1984.1984

Versions of poems in this collection have appeared in various outlets:
"Guinea Pig" and "This Month" appeared in *The Cancer Poetry Project.*
"Snow" appeared in *The Potomac Review.*. "Soul" appeared in *The Comstock
Review.* "Luminous," "Joy," "Fall," "Faith," "Easter," "If" and "Let
Morning Come" appeared in *The Mennonite.*

**Library of Congress Cataloguing-in-Publication Data**
Cadwallader-Staub, Julie, 1957-
Face to face : a poetry collection / Julie Cadwallader-Staub.
  p. cm. -- (Dreamseeker poetry series ; v. 8)
Summary: "Two days after his forth-sixth birthday, Warren Cadwallader-Staub
learned his chronic back pain was caused by multiple myeloma. This poetry col-
lection records the realities of living with someone dying of cancer as well as the
author's journey through death back to her own healing"--Provided by pub-
lisher.
  ISBN-13: 978-1-931038-52-2 (trade pbk. : alk. paper)
  ISBN-10: 1-931038-52-X (trade pbk. : alk. paper)
  1. Cancer--Patients--Family relationships--Poetry. 2. Bereavement--Poetry. 3.
Consolation--Poetry. I. Title.
  PS3603.A374F33 2010
  811'.6--dc22
                              2010017657

17 16 15 14 13 12 11 10    10 9 8 7 6 5 4 3 2 1

*For Warren*

# CONTENTS

# PART 1
# THINKING THE UNTHINKABLE

### THINKING THE UNTHINKABLE

I waited at the
stop sign a long, long time for
the light to turn green.

## PAPER-CUT

I got a nasty paper-cut
right where my writing callus used to be.
It bled; it hurt; it kept opening back up.

I showed it to my daughters.
They said in unison,
"That's no big deal Mom."

I sought out my son.
He just rolled his eyes.

Then I went to you.
You kissed it tenderly.
You told me it would be better soon.
You said to keep a band-aid on it, and not do any dishes—
that I could take some of your morphine if I needed it,
that it looked like I would get by without IV antibiotics.

Me with a paper-cut
You with cancer
It's hard to get any sympathy around here.

## *THE BLESSING OF CHILDREN—1*

On the way to the hospital to visit you,
one daughter observes to the other:
"This road will never be the same."

'Ah,' I think, 'These are the tracks
cancer leaves upon our children's lives.'

But our other daughter replies:
"Yes, I'll never forget
the first day we showed our calves!"

The road to the hospital
also leads to the county fairgrounds.

## IF YOUR EYES

The doorbell quits working.
You recruit our daughter to fix it with you.
You help her take the chime down from the wall,
re-attach the internal wiring,
oil what needs to be oiled.
She shows me how she fixed it.

You come up from the basement:
"Remember how the radiators always clang
when the heat comes on?
Well, I found the pipe that was the problem,
re-pressurized the system.
They won't clang anymore."

Our son comes home with a new oboe concerto.
You sit at the piano to accompany him.
He sight-reads it, *prestissimo*.    *faster than presto*
You manage a few notes, a chord here and there,
but it is too fast, and too beautiful.
You just sit and cry while he plays.

You walk into the bathroom
to brush your unruly red hair,
just as I step out of the shower.
"Whoa!" you say, faking a heart attack.
"Warn me next time!"

If your eyes were not so brown and kind
If your hands were not so warm and knowledgeable
I wouldn't mind your having cancer
I wouldn't mind losing you.

## SOUL

One thing Darwin can't explain
is the sound of the wind in the trees.
The trees gain no advantage
when their leaves rustle and moan.

But when we listen to the wind in the trees,
suddenly we are four-dimensional beings
slipping from our too tight skins
shedding time, priorities, need.

Oh to embrace what we love,
who we are, who we are becoming
Oh to lose fear, to forget its name entirely—
the future is in the tug of our hearts, the wind in the trees:
always upward, outward, bracing and embracing

we rise to the sound.

## FROM DOUBLE-TREE TO SINGLE-TREE

Twenty years ago,
we harnessed ourselves
a well matched pair.
The yoke was light
made of pleasure and promise.
The burden was easy
only dreams in tow
an open road ahead.

Over the miles,
reality's version of our dreams filled our cart:
brown eyed babies
jobs, a home of our own.
We slowed to a walk
pulled, celebrated, sorrowed
side by side.

Now you have fallen and can't get up.
Harness wrecked.
Cart upended.
Children, jobs, lives
spill about us.

For six months I hoped
we might re-place our harness
re-fill our cart
pull together towards our future.

But now I wonder:
How do I right the cart
fill it with dreams still coming true
long-legged teenagers, canoe, books,
computer, oboe, piano, flute, French horn,
mortgage, school work, my job

and you?

And how do I
a tired and grieving mare
pull this cart
now heavy enough
for a team of Belgians?

## GOOD FRIDAY

Jesus' friends betrayed him
ran for cover
abandoned him to ridicule and the cross.

Men hammered blow after blow
into Jesus' living hands,
pierced his open palms
splintered his delicate hand-bones,
until the nails sank deep into solid wood.

They hoisted that cross upright
with Jesus so precariously attached
his hands tearing
his feet buckling.

He cried out.

When I sink to my knees
to weep and pray
Oh, I am grateful
to commune with Him—
not an amorphous god of light or truth—
but a God who reached for us with outstretched arms
vulnerable flesh
defenseless blood
who comforts me with scarred hands
a broken heart
like mine.  husband 'crucified'?

## LUMINOUS

If light traveled only in lines,
not also in waves,
each rising band of world
would have its brief and blasting hour of sun
before rotating into darkness again.

If love traveled only in lines,
not also in waves,
what child could withstand
the impact of a parent's love?
What spouse could survive
that week or month or year
of longing for another?
What believer could summon
sufficient courage
to bow her head and pray?
If love traveled only in lines.

No—we have evolved,
along with all the natural world,
for waves.
So when we are struck with a straight line—
Jesus, for example, or death—
almost everything in us
seeks to silence this intruder
who alone stands impervious to our world of
curve and compromise.

"death is so final"
from 'This Life'

But something deeper whispers:
Don't crucify this stranger.
You could not perceive waves
without a straight line.
In its bright blast of truth,
See what it illuminates.

**IF** *(handwritten)* Face To Face w/ Death

*(handwritten, top right)* "Row, Row, Row your boat gently down the stream ..."

*"Our birth is but a sleep and a forgetting:*
*The Soul that rises with us, our life's Star,*
*Hath had elsewhere its setting,*
*And cometh from afar:"*
—*William Wordsworth*
Ode: 'Intimations of Immortality'

If our birth is but a sleep and a forgetting,
then our death must be an awakening, a remembering.
Listen. Can you discern a long-forgotten melody?
Is exquisite harmony beckoning
from the edges of your memory?
If our death is an awakening, a remembering,
is there a glory beyond the rose, beyond music?
Is there a sweeter spring than the daffodil
in heaven's deepening expanse?

I cannot willingly release you
yet
if we love what we love
because dim memories
evoke such love,
then
death is just a passing
from loving hands to loving hands
from the rose, to the glory beyond the rose,
to a sweeter spring, a richer harmony. . . .

If
our birth is but a sleep and a forgetting.

❖ . . . 26  *(handwritten)* Keeping 'Faith' (IF), not 'certainty'

## SNOW

I have shoveled an acre, a mile, a ton of snow
since November
but still, this last day of March
I lift my face and close my eyes
to feel the first flakes of the latest storm.

I love the snow:

How water rises
from earth's undulating skin,
eluding our senses entirely

how it condenses far beyond our earthly home

makes its singular descent,
carrying its own illumination,

falling light upon light upon light.

## BUFFALO DON'T CARE

Living with cancer cells
coursing through your veins
is like herding buffalo:
You herd them wherever
*they* choose to go.

Only you're not on horseback.
You're staring right into their
dark, uncomprehending eyes.   (*face to face?*)
You're feeling their massive threatening size,   *w/ death*
their incalculable numbers,
overwhelming your little frame.

People tell you incessantly,
'A positive attitude will beat this.'
But you could be Pollyanna on Prozac—
Buffalo don't care.

All the optimism in the world
turns to dust
under their stampeding hooves.
No boot, no smile,
nothing left
but silent, trampled, plains.

# PART 2
# GUINEA PIG

## APPARENTLY

we have two cards to
play: "suffering" and "death." So
suffering is good.

## THIS MONTH

I forgot to pay the mortgage this month.
But I got you to the hospital in time
every time
and I made sure you took your medications
morphine, Compazine, Atavan, Benadryl, Levoflox,
    Imodium
at the right time
every time.
And I finished the school year
for all three kids:
homework, projects, concerts, field trips, award ceremonies.
And I kept up
with my own job.
We got through the first phase of this transplant
and another month of family life
pretty well
this month.

So I called the mortgage company
to explain
why I forgot to pay the mortgage.
I waded through
voice messaging options.
There wasn't one that said
"If you have a reasonable explanation for
forgetting to pay the mortgage, press 2."
So while I listened again,
trying to figure out which option might result in a human
    being,

I trapped the phone against my ear with my shoulder
and checked your temperature.
It was over 101.
I had to hang up.
Call the doctor.
Take you to the hospital.
And forget
that I forgot
to pay the mortgage
this month.

## GUINEA PIG

As if your cancer weren't enough,
the guinea pig is dying.
The kids brought him to me
wrapped in a bath towel
'Do something, Mom.
Save his life.'

I'm a good mom.
I took time from work,
drove him to the vet,
paid $77.00 for his antibiotics.

Now, after the kids rush off to school,
you and I sit on the bed.
I hold the guinea pig, since he bites.
You fill the syringe.
We administer the foul smelling medicine
to this black and white repository of our children's love

hoping the little fellow will live
admitting to each other:
if he doesn't,
it'll be good practice.

## *PEACE WITH HONOR*

My husband says, "You do the 50 cents and I'll do the 75,"
more clearly than anything he's said all day,
but he sleeps on, unaware.
Opening his veins to high dose chemotherapy,
he wages a cell-to-cell war for a few more years.

Outside his little room,
sit twelve people
in twelve recliners
with twelve IVs,
dripping drugs
that kill in order to cure,
destroy in order to save.
But I am thinking: is this our own Vietnam?

Today, when my husband's mind is lost in the jungles,
when his memory has succumbed to guerrilla warfare,
when he is viciously angry at me
because the car door is not in the right place,
I wonder:
can we win a war
in the depths of his marrow,
in the underground passages of his exhausted body,
with these defoliants?

Maybe it's better to die sooner,
with an intact mind
and a decimated body,
than die later,

mind dissolving
body bruised and calloused
by suffering compounded by suffering.

Maybe it's better
to depart Saigon,
christen this ship
with its rightful name:
Death—
And just sail it
as well as we can
into the dying light.

"Do Not go gentle
into that good night"
Dylan Thomas

## FRONTIER

Pity has no place in love
or so I thought,
till Pity came
and staked a claim
on our land.

Pity had no place in love
till you convulsed
from the effort of lying down,
and our land fell
stunned, mute, empty
a sudden desert
where our homestead once stood.

and Pity's claim?
a humble spring
a quiet watering
at home
in this wasteland.

### EVERY STRIDE

The sun streams through bright yellow beech and maple
    trees
their brilliant leaves shift in welcome beneath my feet
pine needles drop through the clear air
and I am running through these woods
breathing in golden
breathing out golden

I love every stride I spring
every root I clear
every branch I duck—
and you.

You whom I have known and loved half my life
You whom I left lying in bed
gray, unmoving
taut with pain
dreaming of dangling naked like a mobile
with nothing to touch your electrified skin but air.

How can we keep living this life of opposites
me running, raking, hugging our children;
you, on fire from the inside out,
despite a dozen painkillers each day?

Surely this world is incomprehensible
ruled by neither reason nor love.

## HOW WE SURVIVE

The day after we found out
you had advanced bone marrow cancer,
our fifteen-year-old son,
wanting French fries from the hospital coffee shop
looked back,
through the nurses and the IVs
and quoted Jim Carrey at you:
"Don't go dying on me now."

Months later,
after your second bone marrow transplant,
you developed shingles.
Even a sheet was too painful against your skin,
let alone pajamas or a bathrobe,
never mind jeans or a Tshirt.
Our twelve-year-old daughter commented,
"Now we're prepared if the roof leaks."

Today, I sit on the side of your hospital bed
watching the antibiotics drip in,
this time combating a blood borne staph infection.
We hear repeated loud thumps from the next room.
"Sounds like they've run out of anesthesia," I say.
"Guess so," you reply.
"Three whacks for an appendectomy,
Four for open heart surgery."

## SISTERS' HANDS

I walked in the woods to find
something, anything
to teach me about suffering:
a twisted tree
a split rock
a leg-hold trap
a dead deer
a metaphor:
something, anything
to explain why pain should inhabit
your every motion, every breath
why you should wake to cry
and sleep to tears,
week after grueling week

why

But instead I saw white pines that rose sixty straight feet
into a clear November sky.
I saw boulders with eight colors of lichens
soaking up the sun.
I saw white oak and red oak leaves
lying side by side like sisters' hands.
But suffering?
No.
Only chipmunks racing around their vast estates
cheeks full, preparing for winter.

## A CLINICAL TRIAL OPENS UP
## ON THE ROAD TO HOSPICE

This road has been hard enough and steep enough already.
My little car has struggled
through potholes, over boulders,
along rocky cliffs, around hairpin turns,
rarely exceeding first gear,
blowing out tires,
losing its exhaust system entirely,
on this unmarked road.

And now, with the inglorious end in sight
—just a huge drop-off—
here's a stop sign
where the incline is the steepest
and I am burning up the clutch
while we pause,
weighing the merits
of accelerating into thin air
or stopping
long enough
to roll backwards
some unknown distance
before starting back up this steep slope—again.

## IF LIFE WERE LIKE TOUCH FOOTBALL

Driving north on Route 2A
from Vermont to Maine
listening to the news:
—the New England Patriots coach was caught
trying to videotape the handsignals of the New York
    Giants—

I remember how we six sisters
would recruit a few boys from the neighborhood
for a pick-up game of touch football in the street,
how we'd break into teams,
huddle around whomever was chosen to be qb,
how the qb would extend her left palm, flat,
into the middle of the huddle,
plant the index finger of her right hand in the center of her
    palm, and then
with finger motions and whispers,
she would diagram who was to go where and when,
in order to so confuse and fool the other team
that one of us could break free
and go long.

Oh that feeling
of running as fast as I could
extending my arms, my hands, my fingers
as far as I could
watching that spiralling bullet of a football,
reminding myself:

if you can touch it,
you can catch it.
If you can touch it,
you can catch it.

## HOPE

Hope is as insidious
as infatuation.
You can try
to reason it away,
ignore it,
beat it into submission,
but hope takes root in the cracks
between today and tomorrow,
sends its tendrils
spiraling upwards,
oblivious to your best efforts,
smiling.

*positive attitude in face of oblivion.*

*resilience*

## CONTRAST

Harsh winter wind whips the air
yanks off the oaks' last leaves,
reveals their morose and reaching branches, dark and skele-
    tal trunks.

But a single white pine floats out its green, voluptuous
    boughs
defying the black forest behind:
in the contrast is the beauty.

Outside the church,
it's just another wretched December night.
People hurry by, each shielded
from slicing wind and snow by a heavy coat,
a straining umbrella.

Yet through our church's arched doorway,
umbrellas snap shut
coats slide off
people exclaim and embrace.
Music, pine, candles fill the air.
Here we bloom, we open toward each other:
in the contrast is the gift.

death, mortality,
Knowing we die to die
makes life sweeter

(in movie Troy Achilles
talks about this (Brad Pitt)

45 . . . ❖

After forty nights of unrelenting pain,
we are able—just tonight—to sleep like spoons.
I can pull your sharp arm around my waist,
lose your thin wrist between my breasts,
hold your bony hand under my chin.
I know, we know, life doesn't have to be this good
this free of pain:

in the contrast lies the joy.

## RECOVERED FROM CHEMO,
## WAITING FOR PROGNOSIS

Do you remember when you were a child
and one morning
the whole world called your name?

You ran outside for the joy of running
from the swingset to the tree to the neighbor's and back,
and then a butterfly in the spring air

caught your eye
and you stopped
and that butterfly

oh, it turned a floating turn.
It alighted on your sleeve.

And you stood still and watched
as it folded and unfolded
closed and opened

its whole being
again and again
while you held your breath

and waited.

### BORROWED TIME

This is the spring I have hoped for:
Your hair is back, more beautiful than before.
I can't see your skeleton anymore.
You can walk, ride your bike, play with the kids
all in the same day.
The monthly test of your tumor load
has been stable for five months in a row.

So what is this sickening dread
this haunting knowledge,
that we are no longer walking
that we stepped on an escalator some time ago
its duration unknown
but its destination certain.

## HOPE THE THING WITH FEATHERS

*Hope is the thing with feathers*
*That perches in the soul.* . . .
—Emily Dickinson XXXII

Oh I would almost return
to those early days
when Hope sang a continuous song.
We would drive your cancer to its knees,
we would make it beg for mercy,
we would annihilate it,
with drugs, prayer, visualization, spinach.

Oh I would almost return
to those early days
when the treatments were as promising
as they were incomprehensible:
VAD, EDAP, tandem stem cell transplant.

But now we are well acquainted with all of them
and well acquainted with grief.

Hope the thing with feathers
has watched with us
as test after test, number after number,
clips its unsuspecting wings,
interrupts its endless song.

Hope now looks back at us with startled eyes
as day after day, week after week,
begins and ends in pain.

Hope now keeps its faltering song within its breast.
Waiting, uncertain, abashed.
    *flustered*

Oh I would almost return
to those early days
when Hope—and you—were fully fledged.
When you and I were confident
that we would never stop,
never stop at all.

## *SOLO*

I am a sprinter caught
in a marathon
I have run for days, for months, and still
I don't know
whether I am at mile 2 or 22.

My heart failed quite a while ago
but my legs go on,
while I fantasize
about jumping outside the traffic cones
slowing to a walk
ducking and disappearing into the onlooking crowd
or, failing that,
sprinting into the path of an oncoming truck
because I know

at the end of this marathon
there is no banner or jubilation.
We will not stumble, happy and relieved,
into our car, and head home for a long shower and nap.
No, the ending of this marathon
is me watching you succumb to death's slow but inexorable
     victory,
and the start of the next marathon—solo—
for me.

## HOW I SURVIVE

Before words, I learned
Nazis killed my Dad's grandmother at Terezin;
before words I knew
he loved her.

Beyond words I learned
my Mom's last baby
was a stillborn son;
beyond words I knew
she loved him.

But if grief formed my bones,
love created my flesh:

Didn't my doctor-father
—though haunted by memories of his childhood in
    Germany—
didn't he battle the bureaucracies here,
bring his skills to inner cities, to Indian reservations, to im-
    migrants and refugees,
one country's outcast
doing what he could for others outcast too?

And didn't my mother
—never forgetting the coldness that filled her
while she carried her last child within her—
didn't she dare
to raise her six daughters
on fresh air and ice cream?

And didn't my parents make all of us
attend their church
to absorb a faith
that encompassed even their grief?

## DAFFODIL

I have noticed the daffodil
in you and in me:
how she rises and rises—
though ice crusts her green edges
though snow settles on her tight buds—
she rises and rises
drawing from last year's ample store
to incarnate sunshine
in this brittle world.

But I want to know
how many months of plodding gray
can the daffodil endure?
How many seasons
before the memory of sunshine grows dim
before her bulb dessicates, disintegrates
opens its chambered womb
to the worms of dirt and despair?
How long for the daffodil
whose first name was joy?

## *LETTER*

You wrote a letter
to a woman you met on the cancer hall:
'After five chemo treatments,
two transplants,
a staph infection,
shingles,
an experimental treatment,
I am still thinking of you,
wondering how you are.
I remember our short talks
amidst the nurses
the IVs
the morphine.'

You received a letter
from her daughter in return:
'I read your letter to my mom.
Loud and clear every word
I spoke into the heavens.
I know she heard you.'

When I read that, I couldn't stop crying.
Someday I too will speak to the sky
trying to reach you.

But you, you just looked into the distance
and said, "No more pain."

⌐ a hanfull of
oxycontin ?

## *WALK*

Today I would walk away my grief
I would walk out my back door
through the deep woods
choose every northerly lane
seek a world that is beautiful, predictable,
trustworthy again

And when I fall down in exhaustion and defeat
I hope some pale green arctic moss
will cushion my face
that the clear calm cold of ice
will numb me
and I will feel this grief no more.

*Life goes on!*

## THE BLESSING OF CHILDREN—2

It was just two nights ago
when we told the kids:

No more treatments for Dad.
The doctors predict three to six months.

So tonight when I go into our daughter's bedroom
to kiss her good night
and she is still wide awake,
I sit down beside her
put my hand on her shoulder
and say
"Is it anything you want to talk about?"

"Oh Mom," she says.
"Tomorrow I have two whole class periods
with that boy who's been smiling at me.
Oh Mom, I just can't wait for tomorrow to come."

## *THE BLESSING OF CHILDREN—3*

My son and I are barreling south through New York City
    on 95,
on our way to his first conservatory audition.
I am hitting every pothole in front of me
but avoiding the continuous concrete barrier on my left
and the roaring trucks on my right.

I am brooding
over my husband's impending death:
how sick will he be by the time I get home in a few days?
will he be okay for our daughters' birthdays in April?
will he live to see our son graduate in June?

Suddenly my son shouts
"Oh my God!
"Look at that! That exit sign says M – I – A – N – U – S !
My anus! Oh my God! There's a town called My Anus!"

"Where do you live?" he begins in one voice.
"I live in My Anus," he answers in another.
"Oh really," he goes on. "Do you know where the fire sta-
    tion is in My Anus?
I found the nicest little antique store in My Anus!
You know, I just can't believe all the great people who live in
    My Anus."

We were still laughing when we came to the bridge.

# PART 3
# LET MORNING COME

## CROSSING THE BAR

You wanted to see the ocean again
—you who grew up with miles of corn fields in every direc-
    tion—
so I drove us to the Cape
and despite gushing nosebleeds
unrelenting tremors
overwhelming tiredness
we walked along the beach
for a few minutes both days
in the soupy fog
staring into the answerless waves
talking about what you loved most
in these not quite five decades of life you've been given.

On the drive home
you stayed awake long enough
to finish planning your memorial service:

*Precious Lord, Take My Hand*
*Great Is Thy Faithfulness*
*In the Bulb There is a Flower*

## COMA

It has been a long Saturday.
So many people wanting to see you.
So many people you wanted to see.
Finally, everyone gone, you throw up
and go to bed for the night.

I massage your feet
as we talk briefly
before the leaden sleep
that has become customary
takes you away:

"Wake me up for church in the morning."
"Let's wait and see how you feel."
"No, wake me up. I want to go to church."
"But it might be better for you to rest instead."
"No, wake me up. Promise me."
"Okay. I will."
"Promise?"
"Yes, I promise."

I tried.
Many times.

## HOMEWARD

Do you remember
decades ago
how eagerly we awaited
the birth of our first child?

He could not have known,
turning in the womb,
how we longed to feel his weight in the crooks of our arms
to count his curling fingers and stubby toes
to welcome him home.

He could not have imagined
air, a kiss, a birthday cake, laughter.

Yet when he peered at us through his newborn eyes
it was like meeting like
love meeting love.

Now, it is your turn.
Still anchored to this world
you cannot imagine an existence
without gravity or grain elevators,
without breathing or breakfast,
without a love that relies on fingertips, mouths, hands.

Yet we believe
that such angels as do exist
are waiting to welcome you:
that life is a homeward journey,
and you are almost there.

## *BREATH*

Lord, please pay attention
look at him, now, quickly, while this lasts.
See how peaceful he is
his brow as clear as a perfect note
his whole body relaxed
as if he were already resting
in the palm of your hand.

But now, watch him now, he needs to breathe.
See how his whole body contorts!
His face in such a grimace!
Listen to that awful sound he makes,
that desperate, hauling, grasping for air!

Lord, I love this man
I have loved him more than half my life
and this agony is happening
for him
for me
every few seconds
I am calling hospice
asking the nurse to come right now
asking if we can give him more morphine

But please
talk to me while we wait.
I am standing at the intersection of love and death
finding that all roads
lead in the same direction.

## LET MORNING COME
### (after "Let Evening Come" by Jane Kenyon)

Let the owl
be satisfied at last and return
to his snowy bower.

Let the orange rim of the sun
grab hold of the horizon
and hoist itself
into a new day.

Let the eastern faces of the trees
warm up with light.
The chickadee emerge.
The snow throw off its blue cloak.
Let morning come.

To the mice huddled in the nest:
his searchlight eyes are closing,
his killing talons harmless now
clasped around a branch.

To the water caught in ice:
remember your sweet song of motion,
your lithe and liquid body?
Let the melting begin.

To the bulb aching in the ground:
Now, now is the time for rising.
Now, now is the time to flower.

Listen, can you hear it too?
God is calling.
Let morning come.

## WHAT I HATED MOST

was not the way the hospice nurse
changed your bed that last day:
the way she pushed your body up on to one side,
ripped the soiled sheets from underneath you,
rammed the new sheets along your upturned back,
then hauled you over the humped up sheets
so she could spread them and tuck them
and flop your body back down flat again.

I did not hate that the most,
even though you gathered
what scraps of consciousness you had left,
to say "no" to her,
and then "No no no no no."

As it turned out what I hated most
happened the next morning
after the funeral home guys put your body on their gurney,
after they rolled that gurney
into the back of their van,
after they crouched there to snap
the gurney into its place on the floor,
first one side, then the other, and
it racked your body
first one way,
and then the other

and there was no one
no one
to hold your head.

## COMFORT

I remember the nights
that your cancer
defeated me:

how I would hold it together
through the last evening rituals:
walking the dog
kissing our children good night
taking my shower

how I would slide into bed beside you,
you fast asleep,
put my hand on your thin chest,
and cry.

And eventually—
the rising and falling of your chest
the inhaling and exhaling of your breath
the warmth of your body in our bed—
would soothe me to sleep.

I could use that now.
I could use that now.

## ALMOST FIFTY

I am almost fifty
and this person I am becoming
—the height and depth and breadth of me—
is infused with sorrow.

Even my love, especially my love,
for our children
is full of the weight of loss
for the loving and silly father you were to them.

Still I will not worship grief,
let it curdle into bitterness,
let it define my days.

When I close my eyes
and see your face
—whether it is brimming with life
or stilled in death—
it bears the same message:
"Wear shoes that sparkle.
Go into the greening world.
Carry me as long as you need to.
But let me be light for you.
Let me be light."

## FALL

I am losing the fight against mold in the shower.
Every crack in the sidewalk has filled up with weeds—again.
Despite twenty years of reminders,
I still find my children's socks
in the living room.
Oh well.

Then there's you.
Remember how gladly we poured
every hope, prayer, drug, vitamin into you
and still—we lost you.

Still—you are gone.

Everything disintegrates.

Which is why
when I run in the woods in the morning,
when I walk the dog at night
I listen:
the geese are migrating.

Far below the perfect constellations,
they call to each other.

Far below the perfect constellations,
they navigate
by the heavens.

## *UNTITLED*

Thank you God
for this sling
of a hammock
that holds my life
like the broken arm it is
without his love.

## *FAMILY REUNION*

Mom and Dad

Doris and Lloyd
Joanie and Andy
Barb and Buck
Julie
Nancy and David
Mimi and John

## CIRCLE

Consider the circle
The rose
The face
The sun

Consider the circle
The bullethole
The pit
The whirlpool

Every day which shall it be
The spiraling inward into despair
The reaching outward towards the rounding world?

## ONE FOOT

I am learning
how
to skate
backwards
to balance
on
one
foot
while
ska
ting backwards
to center my weight over only one blade
to do cross
overs while skating
back
wards

to trust

one ankle
one foot
one blade

I am
lear
ning

## BLESSING

I awoke with a rainbow in my hand

a ray of sun might have angled through a raindrop and my
    open window
to create the soft colors in my curled palm

But more likely
I opened my eyes
just a moment before God expected me to
and I glimpsed Her
resting there.

## GRIEF —1

Listen:
to understand glaciers,
you need to learn a whole new language.

How snow collects in cirques, *deep walled basin on a mountain forming the head end of a valley.*
how its own sheer tonnage
compresses, transforms the delicate flakes into ice,
and how the ice—
propelled only by its own heaviness—
starts to move.

There is the brittle surface ice;
there is the massive viscous ice flowing
unseen beneath it.    *syrupy*

Along the bottom of the glacier
the frost wedging, cracking, booming
is so effective, the *roches moutonnées,*
the drumlins, have no choice    *oval hill of glacial drift.*
but to be changed, even as they are left behind.
    *Accumulation of earth & stone*
And the moraine, the erratics? — *boulder transported by Glacier*
Watch how the glacier picks them up,
carries them for years.
How it drops them miles from home
in its great melting wake.    — *short mound of stratified drift*
How the eskers, kames and kettles *steep sided hollow.*
combine to create    *long narrow ridge of boulders*
a whole new landscape
as the glacier finally dissipates
across its stratified outwash plain.

## GRIEF—2

If you swim in this ocean
as if in a pool,
stroke by stroke by stroke,
—your destination fixed in your mind's eye—
you will soon tire, fade
and be cast on the sand                 *like the heroine of*
with the other crushed                   *Kate Chopin's Awakening*
things of the deep.

But if you approach this ocean
forgetting everything you know about swimming
and rely only
on your own buoyancy,      *high spirits? resilience?*

you will feel the strength,    *Buddhists say don't stop the*
the immensity,                        *feeling, let it wash over you.*
the depth of each wave,        *And be mindful of how it*
its dark and drowning power.   *makes your body feel.*

It will lift you up,
encase you in its powerful grip
for its own time
then let you go
sometimes gentle
sometimes harsh
again and again and again.

Your whole notion of destination fades away:
floating, you realize
this ocean is your destination,
each wave your teacher
for now
for now
for now.

*like a mermaid?*

*see my poem "Awakening"*

### *NO STEROIDS NO DOCTORS*
### *NO TERMINAL DIAGNOSIS*

I woke up this morning thinking of the laundry
and how pleasant
to have such a small thought,
such an easy thing,
be my earliest companion.

Then I got up and pulled on the bathrobe
that he gave to me, and I was
grateful for its warmth
thankful also that it reminded me only of his lanky em-
    brace,
the way his long arms wrapped around me
like a reflex.

## BECAUSE
### After "Peaches" by Li Young Lee

Because death hovers in the background,
I leave work early
lie in the hammock
and sleep in the September sun.
Happy.

All afternoon, as I snooze
my heart presses against its own scar tissue
straining the new seams
so much love
so much loss

When I awake, I am dotted
with dragonflies and pine needles.
I am loving the skin and the shade,
the sugar and the days,
because

I can still feel the whoosh
of death's smashing fist
when it nailed the guy
right next to me. *her husband.*

*In movie Troy
Achilles says gods envy humans
because life is so short &
so much more intense.*

**AND**

My life is as heavy and incomprehensible
as that boulder
—think of a well loved husband and father
dead before fifty—

<u>and</u>　= both true

My life is as light and joyful
as that butterfly
who slipped from her shell of duty
to find
her own way.

## THROUGH A GLASS DARKLY

Lord, I know that You created
these sumptuous banks of golden rod
nodding in the wind.
Yours too are the wild grapes
cascading from their dense tangle of vines,
and the bright jewelweed that beckons from the creek bed,
the jewelweed that bursts open at the merest touch
flinging its seeds into the late summer air.

But tell me about this chasm of emptiness within me
that I can neither illuminate nor fill. *depression?*
Tell me about the thickening fog
overtaking my brother-in-law's brain,
rendering him at age 58
unable to remember how to open the car door
or why he shouldn't seek sex with a prostitute.
Tell me about the young girl
whose face got in the way
of a nail bomb,
and the young man
who looked around that mosque
—perhaps seeing her—
and still detonated himself.

Lord, I know all this is within
the great circle of your love,
but I bow my head at the mystery of it:
how a world so beautiful
can hold so much cruelty and sorrow.

### GRIEF—3

All winter: crows and chickadees.
Now, standing in this snowy field,
I bow my head to untangle the joyful calls:
goldfinches, kingbirds, robins, cedar waxwings.

And I can hear the snow melting too:
the caves, pillars, ridges, layers,
these many-storied crystalline structures
known only to winter
collapsing under their own weight.

In spring, even grief struggles
to maintain its icy mansion.
Faith breathes upon its very foundation
and when the ice gives way, room by roof by *porte cochére*:
well, look, it was made of water too:

the same water that birthed us
the same water that sustains us
the same water that this goldfinch,
is splashing in right now,
its plumage turning from olive to gold.

*(handwritten:)* "sweet smell of Spring
lures me away
from all of this"

from
my
Nobody's
Perfect

### EMPTY NEST

For the love of summer,
I hang the clothes on the line
marveling at how
the man underwear disappeared
and now it's been years;

how the boy underwear
went from dinosaurs to boxers
and now has flown off
to college and young adulthood;

how the girl underwear
began as Carter's and is now Victoria's,
and is on the cusp of doing the same, leaving

only my own underwear to populate
this long line holding years of swimming suits,
towels, sheets, memories snapping in the breeze.

For the love of summer,
I make strawberry rhubarb pies
weaving the lattice crust
over and under, back and forth,
thinking of how I never had time to make pies
when my husband was living,
imagining how he would have appreciated them.

For the love of summer,
I drive to the lake,
swim out past the raft,
past the buoys,
loving the sun, the waves,
the open expanse before me,

also the shore,
the years.

## WINDOW

It is morning, and
the whole world is here – again.

Who knows where this wind has been
before rushing past my window?
Has it raced above the blue whales sustained by tiny krill,
drifted past the python, draped and waiting in the rainfor-
    est,
sent the singing fruit bat on its night-time mission,
carried the warbling vireo's song northward?

And the rain is coming—I can smell it in the air.
Perhaps it has already passed over the ancient glaciers,
dimmed miles of forests and fields and towns,
perhaps it is rushing right now across the ocean to our east,
dappling the twining sand roses as they uncurl across the
    dunes,
teasing the bees who seek the season's first pollen.

Soon it will be here to soak this opening earth,
to make the subterranean aquifers sing,
to fill the ephemeral vernal pools
so fairy shrimp and water striders,
mole salamanders and wood frogs,
can heed their ancestral calling
and hatch another spring.

## OCTOBER

Let me take you
to where the milkweed grows.
We will walk through the forest
to the field that rises to the east
and there, on the hillside
are dozens.

One has already broken open.

All through the summer I have watched her
rising, expanding, offering
her green and bending body
to the one thing in the world
that can't live without her.

And now that it is October,
those caterpillars are the monarchs
migrating over her head
and now it is her turn,

now she is releasing into the open air
that which she has labored over
through the long days and nights of summer.

It is the only thing I want to do:
enough gossamer to catch the imagination and be carried
    away   silky webs
enough seed to land, to catch hold, to root, to grow.

## SPANNING THE DISTANCE

I am kneeling at the edge
of all tenderness and compassion
praying "Yes" and "Oh my"
for I rambled in the woods again this morning
with sixteen inches of new snow
and I could see
how the first flakes spanned the small distances
between needles, between twigs, between each other
so that their multitudes of sisters and brothers
could build pillows and towers and long reaching arms of
    glory.

The sun rose past one bank of clouds
and, before disappearing into the next,
shot its rays into the forest
and oh what a cacophony
of clarity and brilliance erupted
each snowflake claiming and proclaiming the sudden light
from the glistening snow beside my boots
to the shimmering boughs far above my head
forming a cathedral
—including the clouds
including the blue beyond the clouds—
a cathedral of light.

*came out of the
valley of the
shadow of Death!
Momentarily*

## TURNING THE PAGE

Last night my friend—
a widow for almost a year—
described the way she found her husband
on the kitchen floor
slumped against the cabinets.
How after thirty years of loving
she went to him,
helped him into a more comfortable position
smoothed his hair
closed his eyes.

All day long, I think of her as
I remember the yellow birches.
They stand,
a modest pair,
where one pathway meets another
deep in these Vermont woods.

After a long night of rain
they stood glowing
in the meager January light
as if the rain on the outside,
saturating their golden and curling skin,
had filled them with light on the inside.

And isn't this what life is about
to see beneath the surface
that light radiates into the world even in a January rain;
that love reaches across death,
that love makes death
just another chapter in a very long story.

## *GRATITUDE*

Perhaps you have watched the horse
unlock her long legs
drop her strong body
into the sweet pasture
and roll back and forth, forth and back
until, in a great thrashing
of outstretched neck
kicking hooves
whipping tail,
she twists all the way over
and scrambles back to her feet
stamping, prancing, neighing
her satisfaction with herself and with life,
her great animal joy in the day.

Sometimes I don't know what to do
with this unfamiliar upwelling of joy
like on this April morning
waking up to snow falling,
brightening the trees,
animating the air
and I can hear the sudden song of the house finch
mixed in with the chickadees.

Oh I want to open my heart and join in its sparkling song.
I want to drop to my knees with the horse in the field
and thank the Lord
that I have survived.

## JOY

Who could need more proof than honey—

How the bees with such skill and purpose
enter flower after flower
sing their way home
to create and cap the new honey
just to get through the flowerless winter.

And how the bear with intention and cunning
raids the hive,
shovels pawful after pawful into his happy mouth,
bats away indignant bees,
stumbles off in a stupor of satiation and stickiness.

And how we humans can't resist its viscosity,
its taste of clover and wind,
its metaphorical power:
we yearn for a land of milk and honey
we call our loved ones "honey"

all because bees just do, over and over again, what they were
    made to do.

Oh, who could need more proof than honey
to know that our world
was meant to be

and

was meant to be
sweet?

## PSALM 8

Every day for years
I have walked to the crest of this hill
and turned around to stand still and look west
over the field
across the forest
to the rumpled shoulders of the Adirondacks
now turning from sparkling white
to the browns and blues of earliest spring.

From the tiny clover leaves unfolding at my feet
to the robin singing at the rising sun behind my back,
I wonder: Who are we that You should be mindful of us?
We are such a sorry race
given to fear and greed and selfishness
yet you have given us this world
saturated with water
brimming with light
smelling of pine trees and the opening earth.

## CATERPILLAR

Here is the humble caterpillar.
Look at him rippling towards that twig.
Watch how he attaches himself to it,
binding himself to what he knows he needs.

What is it about this attachment    *Jesus Christ )*
that allows him to give over
his known and sturdy body,
his known and sturdy world?

See how he dissolves
from all he knows
into all he doesn't know;
from all that he now is
into all that he is becoming;
how his body accomplishes
what our minds can scarcely imagine.

Here is the humble caterpillar:

He has lived his whole life
on milkweed plants
one foot above the ground.

Now, he lives his whole life floating
from breeze to breeze
from flower to flower
from nectar to nectar

finally flying from Vermont
where I live
to Mexico
where I have never been.

Anything is possible in this world.

## The Author

Julie Staub was born in Minneapolis, Minnesota. She grew up with her five sisters, her parents and a dog beside one of Minnesota's small lakes. Her favorite words to hear growing up were, "Now you girls go outside and play."

In 1979, Julie graduated from Earlham College (a Quaker college in Richmond, Ind.), with a degree in Religious Studies. At Earlham, she had the good fortune of rooming with a Jane Cadwallader from Iowa, who introduced Julie to her big brother, Warren. They were married in a Quaker ceremony in 1979, had three children, and moved to Vermont in 1992, where they joined the Burlington Friends Meeting (Quaker) and then the College Street Congregational Church (United Church of Christ) in 1995. Julie and Warren Cadwallader-Staub were married for twenty-three years, until his death from multiple myeloma at age forty-nine.

Julie earned a Masters of Social Work degree at Rutgers University. She has served as executive director of the Maternity Care Coalition of Philadelphia, the Vermont Campaign to End Childhood Hunger, and the Child Care Fund of Vermont. She was the vice president for community grantmaking at the Vermont Community Foundation before taking her current position, as the Grants Director for the Burlington School District. Her poems have been featured on Garrison Keillor's "The Writer's Almanac," published in several journals, and included in anthologies. She was awarded a Vermont Council on the Arts grant for poetry in 2001. This is her first collection.

CPSIA information can be obtained at www.ICGtesting.com
Printed in the USA
LVOW070251201011

251307LV00001B/224/P